The
New Slave Ship

Melvin Farmer

Published by
Milligan Books

Formatting/Cover Design

By Chris Ebuehi - Graphic *O*ptions

Published and Distributed by:
Milligan Books
an imprint of
Milligan Books
1425 W. Manchester, Suite B,
Los Angeles, California 90047
(213) 750-3592

First Printing, January, 1998
10 9 8 7 6 5 4 3 2 1

ISBN 1-881524-18-3

Acknowledgement

All praises are really due to God. I was taken in through the back door, but because of Jesus. I was let out the front. To my moms, what can I say? I love you and this book is dedicated to you for the dedication you've given to me. Before I left for prison, my mother was a picture of perfect health; now she's on five different medications. Mom, keep your head up and your faith high. To the staff and all my friends at St. Andrew Park, thanks for the many late nights of taking me home and feeding me when I was broke. My "go to" guy, Jay, much love and respect for giving me the right thing and keeping me above water during hard times.

Now, for my people on the other side of the fence, to all homeboys on Death Row at San Quentin State Prison - Big Tookie, Evil, Treach, C.W., Lavelle, Chico, Danny, and Freaky Pete - keep the faith. To the fellas walking the main-line, and to those in the hole, I haven't forgotten the promise that I gave before I left. I'm still staying down for the struggle and the injustice that's being put down. So please quit dirty macking me for not writing back. Business was at hand.

Also, to my second family in Madera County, thanks for the support. To all the Farmers in my bloodline, peace. To the three M's in my life-Melvin, Marcel, and Melanie-I wasn't there in the past, but I'm here for the future. Much love. Finally to my publisher, Milligan Books, thanks for giving me an opportunity to express and voice my thoughts.

Love and respect to all,

Melvin Farmer

PREFACE

Today, we are witnesses to a new high-tech slave trade. This new slave ship is known to many as "prison." The only difference in this slave ship is that it does not sail. Black men, Black women, and even Black children who are now tried as adults, are packed into this ship (cell) like sardines, and they are treated like animals, not humans. In fact, they are treated worse than animals. Animals are given more protection under the law than are Blacks in America.

Does America really want to put an end to crime? I don't think so. Crime pays big money for those who invest in the expanding correctional industrial complex. Who is really making money from crime? Is it the dope dealers, the carjackers or the burglars? I don't think so. Profits from crime are lining the pockets of large corporations. Companies once engaged in the cold war have now joined the scramble for penal dollars.

Let's just look at a few examples of those who profit from crime. There are the private prison operators, the companies who build and supply prison cells, those who supply medicine and medical supplies, and the food providers. A profit is being made on everything from a toothpick to a washing machine. Economically deprived towns are fighting over having a prison or two constructed, so their town can have a source of jobs, building of new homes and new businesses, and support for existing businesses.

Once again, every Black man, Black woman and Black children is being viewed as a precious commodity - a money-making machine. I can hear the auctioneers, the large corporations, saying, "Can I get a bid? Can I get a bid?"

Today, there is a better crop of slaves to choose from. Potential owners are no longer fighting over the slave who can produce more babies or the one who is the strongest. Now intellect is in demand. Corporations demand professional skills, and the minds of doctors, lawyers, politicians, ministers, leaders, engineers, computer analysts, etc. Intellectually inclined Negroes are more in demand because large corporations can downsize, and at the same time earn more profit, by contracting nearly free labor from prison workers.

Isn't it ironic that, at the same time that the government is saying "cut the welfare checks and make them work," American workers are losing their jobs to prison workers? What's up with this?

To assure stability of return on prison stock market investments, politicians are creating harsher penalties and creating new laws. Democrats and Republicans both push legislation in Congress to allow children as young as thirteen years of age to be tried as adults. The mandatory minimum sentences will certainly help to protect investment in prison markets. California constructed eighteen facilities in the last ten years, and expects to construct another twenty-six by the year 2000. Some cities are constructing new facilities for juveniles who have been charged as adults in violent crimes.

Dr. Rosie Milligan made the following observations

regarding the prison industry in her book entitled, <u>Nigger</u>
<u>Please:</u>

Unfortunately, in America one's guilty or innocent verdict is predicated upon the depth of one's pocket. We witnessed the power of money as the "Dream Team" punched holes in the prosecution's evidence. They were able to take the time to probe because O.J. had money to pay for their time.

The plea bargain system is the worst system ever invented. It only brings profit to lawyers who take all they can get from a person, then they suggest a plea bargain. Even though they do not go to trial for you, they never refund monies nor do the victims realize that they have a right to a partial refund. The state saves money because they do not have to incur the expense of proving one's guilt. Are more Blacks in Jail because they commit more crimes? No, more Blacks are in jail because they lack the finances to prove their innocence; therefore, they plea bargain. More Blacks are in jail because they are framed and set up by their paid protectors, the police. Are Blacks a new valuable commodity? Who profits from the new slaves? Bail bond business is certainly reaping its share. Lawyers are reaping their share and the prisons are BIG, BIG business for the future.

Crime and prison construction are big business in America. It is a modern-day form of cotton picking, a legitimate way to practice slavery. Prisons help the economy. Prisons keep white folk who would otherwise be displaced in good jobs. Prisons, by design, will become the leading industry in America. Does our government want to focus more on crime prevention? I don't think so. Will the prison industry become a future place of employment for Black men? I don't think so, because their criminal records will prevent them from obtaining such employment.

Most Blacks who have been incarcerated have difficulties

securing employment, regardless of their education and skills. If you couple the employment dilemma, with the parole and probation stipulation, a revolving door for Black inmates is the result. By now you should understand why the prison industry will soon lead the stock market. Full restitution for the criminal's victims is mandatory and is also a part of the probation plan. One can violate probation by not paying restitution. Blacks have quite a dilemma.

*Is there a reason that Newt Gingrich is focusing on crimes committed by Blacks and not on crimes committed by whites. Is anybody keeping up with what crimes are committed by whites? Are statistics on white crimes being published anywhere? Then one must ask the question, **do whites commit crimes?***

Let us take a close up look at Blacks and crime allegations.

There has been a historical pattern of false evidence; witnesses, due to greed, are being coerced and rewarded for lying under oath; fingerprints are forged. As a result our mothers, father, sons daughters, sisters and brothers are executed or incarcerated for life. Too many, such as Eula Mae Love, Rodney King, Oliver Beasley and Sonji Danese Taylor are beaten, maimed, and slaughtered before ever standing trial.

William Henry Hance, an African-American, was convicted of murder in Muscogee County, Columbus, Georgia by eleven white jurors. The twelfth juror, Gayle Daniels, an African-American, did not cast her vote for the death penalty. The eleven white jurors felt compelled to vote for the death penalty, and in their desperation to get a unanimous vote, forged the African-American juror's signature. During the entire trial, comments were made by some of the white jurors such as, "The nigger should fry," and "That would be one less to breed on the street." The District Attorney was made aware of this fact ten days before Hance's execution but refused to take action. He was like a shark who had already smelled blood. On March 31, 1994, William Henry Hance was executed by a racist-tainted jury deliberation.

In Los Angeles in 1974, Clarence Chance and Benny Powell were tried and convicted and sentenced to life in prison for the killing of David Andrews, an off-duty sheriff's deputy who was gunned down at a gas station at Exposition and Normandie in South-Central Los Angeles. They served seventeen years in the California prison system for a crime they never committed. Because of the public out-cry and effort, Mr. Chance and Mr. Powell's cases were reopened. The false evidence that took away their freedom for seventeen years is yet another example of how the judicial system is failing Blacks.

On February 15, 1994, Channel 7, KABC reported on the 6:30 evening news that police officers in the states of New York, California, Tennessee, Alabama, Arizona, Oklahoma and Georgia forged fingerprints and arrested innocent African-Americans. In October 1990, Shirley Kinge, a 58-year-old African-American woman, was tried and convicted of one of the most brutal murders in New York's history. Salesman Tony Harris, his wife, and two children were blindfolded, shot and set on fire. Police officer David Harding, investigating the case was so desperate for credit for solving the crime that he forged Ms. Kinge's fingerprints from a glass at a restaurant, to the gasoline can found at the scene of the murder. As a result, Ms. Kinge was convicted of arson and burglary, then sentenced to 22 to 60 years in prison. She served two and a half years before state law enforcement authorities learned what had happened and freed her. Ms. Kinge, now past 60, suffered great pain. She says nothing can give her back the time she lost.

February 24, 1994, The Commercial News, Danville, Illinois, reported that police officers in Los Angeles, Chicago and Atlanta were found guilty of planting drugs on African

Americans, causing many innocent men and women to be arrested and given long prison sentences.

The following is a close-up look at the incarceration status:

The number of Black men in federal or state prisons or local jails rose one hundred-thirty percent from 1985 to 1995. In 1985 the number was 309,800. In 1995 the number was 711,600. Keep in mind that Blacks only constitute twelve percent of the United States population.

The number of White men in federal or state prison or local jails rose ninety percent. In 1985 the number was 382,800; in 1995 the number was 726,500.

The number of Black women in federal or state prisons or local jails rose nearly two-hundred percent from 1985 to 1995. In 1985 the number was 19,100; in 1995 the number was 55,300.

The number of White women in federal or state prisons or local jails in 1985 was 21,400; the number in 1995 was 57,800.

Black women in 1994 represented eighty-two percent of the women sentenced for crack cocaine offenses.

DRUG OFFENDERS IN STATE PRISONS

The number of Black people incarcerated on drug charges from 1985 to 1995 accounted for forty-two percent of the total growth among Black inmates.

- The number of Black drug offenders in 1985 was 16,600.
- The number of Black drug offenders in 1990 was 83,400.
- The number of Black drug offenders in 1995 was 134,000.
- The number of White drug offenders in 1985 was 21,200.
- The number of White drug offenders in 1990 was 61,000.
- The number of White drug offenders in 1995 was 86,100.

PERCENTAGE CHANGE FROM 1985 TO 1995 WAS: Blacks 707%; Whites 306%

The media set the American people up to accept the mandatory minimum sentence without question. Most Black movies are loaded with Blacks committing violent crimes.

Major newspapers nationwide carry front-page stories about Blacks and crime. An article in Business Week entitled "The Economics of Crime" in the December 13, 1993 issue stated the following: "Crime is an American tragedy, especially for Blacks. African Americans are disproportionately both perpetrators and victims of criminal violence."

INTRODUCTION

In March of 1994, I became the first victim in Madera County, California to be charged under the three strike mandatory sentencing law. I also hold the distinction of being the first three strike victim to be released from a California state prison on a three strike reversal, and the only one as of this writing

After being incarcerated for three years and eight months, as a result of wrongful arrest, my conviction was overturned. I was released from prison on September 19, 1997. I would like to say that I became a free man on that date; however, I find it hard to use the words "free man" since my fate, like many, is determined by the powers that be. You see, I like many others, I was wrongfully arrested, for a crime I did not commit. Evidence that could have proven my innocence was destroyed and I was imprisoned. I am not a free man. I was granted the privilege to de-board the modern-day slave ship or better known as "prison." Should I encounter any more trouble, or if I am framed again, a minimum sentence of thirty-four years to life awaits me.

The question is, do I lock myself up in my home and never come out or do I try to live and enjoy life as other individuals do?

Every time I eat, every time I walk outside, every moment I spend with my mother and family, every time I go to church, in everything I do that represents happiness and freedom of choice, I am saddened in spirit because of those men that I have left behind. I am not talking about murderers and violent crime offenders. I see the faces of those men who have committed crimes such as stealing a piece of ham on Thanksgiving Day, riding a stolen bicycle, receiving stolen goods, etc. - petty crimes. I also see the faces of those charged with murder and violent crimes who had been framed, and those who accepted a plea-bargain for fear of being framed.

I remember the excitement I felt when I first received notice that I would soon be de-boarding the slave ship. How do you share the excitement of going home with men who are in prison for life? These inmates are being confined in an 8' x 10' stand-up grave (called a cell), and most of their hours are spent rotting away like wood in salt water.

The inmates that I left behind asked me not to forget about them. I gave my solemn oath that I would do my best to make the public aware of the inmates who are getting their lives taken away by the three strike law. I cannot forget about those inmates I left behind. I see their faces, I hear their voices. If you want to know what it was like on the slave ship that our forefathers talked about, just catch a three strike case, and you will soon discover that the difference between the slave ship of your forefathers and today's prison, is that the prison ship does not sail.

I have a heavy burden on my shoulders. My fellow inmates' voices are silenced by the walls that keep them locked up, and it is up to me and to all those who believe in justice, to do what we can to expose the prison crisis and make the public aware that these are human beings behind these walls.

What would happen if the public got news that the employees who work for the dog pound were abusing the dogs? How much longer would the abuse continue? But

Introduction

does human life have as much value? Or could it be that the lives of Blacks and minorities have no value?

Most of America thinks prisoners are no longer human. You even hear Black people saying, "Just get those Bloods and Crips out of our neighborhood; we don't care what you do with them."

Are prisons designed as a means of population control?

Is the denial of conjugal visits for inmates with life sentences designed to curtail the birth rate?

Are prisons the new stock market for a nation of greed?

Is it a coincidence that our military bases were downsizing at the same time that prison construction was on the rise - at the same time that the three strike law was passed - and at the same time of the welfare was reformed - at the same time jobs were being shifted to Mexico - and at the same time of Affirmative Action was dismantled?

Marvin Gaye asked the question in song years ago, "What's going on?" He further stated, "It makes me want to holler and throw up both my hands." Well, I cannot throw up my hands because the faces and voices I left behind haunt me daily.

Dr. Roland Jefferson, a Los Angeles-based African

American forensic psychiatrist, exposed this modern-day slave ship in a work of fiction twenty years ago in his book, *The School on 103rd Street.* Dr. Jefferson once asked these questions, "Do Blacks have a justified reason to be paranoid? Is paranoia only embodied in the psyche of the Black underclass?" *The School On 103rd Street*, a work of fiction seen through a prophetic mind, sheds light on the fact that the constant fear of imminent annihilation is held not only by the African American underclass, but by Black scholars, Black political leaders and the Black middle-class.

Mr. & Mrs. Doctor, Mr. & Mrs. Lawyer, educator, politician, preacher, mayor, Mr. & Mrs. Good Law-Abiding Citizen, please hear my cry today. Neither you nor your children are exempt. Please help me to help those I left behind. Remember the cell that I left yesterday could be your cell, or your child's cell, tomorrow.

The
New Slave Ship

A SHIP THAT DOES NOT SAIL

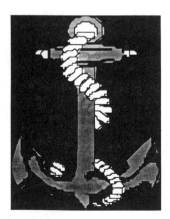

CHAPTER

1

MY PRISON ENCOUNTER

My Prison Encounter

I was sentenced to thirty four years to life for the sale of less than a gram of rock cocaine. I was the first three strike case in Madera County, California. My saga began on March 15, 1994 and ended on September 19, 1997. I had served three years and eight months of my sentence before my conviction was overturned by the California State Court of Appeal, 5th District.

I didn't have a clue about what I would face at my arraignment. When I was told that I could receive a life term for my offense, I knew that there had to be a mistake. I remember asking the attorney, "What are they talking about? What is this new law they're talking about?" You see, I knew the penalty for the crime; the charge, as I knew it, carried 5-8 years upon conviction. I suddenly realized that this was no joke and that my life as a free man was at stake. At that moment, reality began to sink into my brain. My whole life flashed before me.

I remembered a story told to me by a friend who had nearly drowned. As he was going down for the third time, he remembers thinking, "How will my mother handle this?" He saw his children's faces. He thought about all he had accomplished and all he had accumulated in material possessions. This reminded me of an old biblical saying — "For what is a man profited if he shall gain the whole world and lose his own soul?" Then I thought, "What does it profit a man to acquire these material things and go to jail and lose it all?" When I say lose it all, I really do mean lose it all.

The attorney explained to me that if convicted, I would be sentenced under the new three strike mandatory minimum sentence law. I forced myself to calm down. I realized that I must begin planning to save myself. I started collecting evidence that could lead to my freedom. I held on to every piece of paper pertaining to my case.

I became very paranoid. I did not trust anyone in the court system; I had had six different attorneys on this case, and each one was declared to have a "conflict of interest." I had been in Madera County Jail for one year while going through the court system. While they were rushing me to trial, I never had a stable defense because I had no attorney! The writing was on the wall. I now had a new public defender for my case. My trial date was one and one-half months away.

I was sadly mistaken in thinking that the courts would look into my allegations of police misconduct. After all, I had been framed. The district attorney was not playing, and the courts were determined to prove to me that my butt would wear out before the fence would. As expected, I was found guilty. I was braced for this outcome, so this wasn't a sad period for me. I just hated to tell my family. It was clear to me that I would be sentenced to twenty-five years to life; however, my sentence carried a twist. I was given an additional nine years, to run consecutive to my twenty-five-years-to-life sentence. So upon completion of serving my twenty-five-years-to-life sentence, I would have an additional nine years to serve.

CHAPTER

2

A NORMAL DAY FOR THE INMATE WITH A LIFE SENTENCE

After sentencing, I was rushed out of Madera County to Wasco State Prison for evaluation. This is a tedious process. You are awakened at 3 o'clock in the morning, carted out almost naked and put on a van. You're riding in the middle of nowhere and suddenly whoomp, there it is — a slave ship on land (prison).

There are special buildings that house the three strike lifers. With the three strike law, the increase in the number of convicts with life has caused the Department of Corrections to have buildings designated to house "lifers" only.

There were approximately two hundred inmates in the

wing where I was placed. We all had one thing in common; we were receiving more time than inmates who had committed murder.

I started questioning inmates as to the reasons for their twenty-five-years-to-life sentences. The reasons were unbelievable, such as:

One man stole a piece of ham on Thanksgiving Day. One man was riding a stolen bicycle (receiving stolen property).

A stolen shirt was found in one man's house.

One man was a passenger in a stolen car.

The blues would set in at night. If you had the capacity to think, you would think at night. At nighttime I began my soul searching. I asked myself how I could have gotten myself in such a predicament whereby my life had been taken away from me. It was unreal. It was like a movie or show that I did not want to see because the price of admission was too high.

My cellie and I were sent to Lancaster State Prison. When we arrived, the prison was full. We were sent to Administrative Segregation (The Hole) until bed space became available. When we entered the Rotunda, we witnessed a man who had tape around his waist and both his hands. His feet were shackled and a muzzle had been placed over his mouth. My cellie asked me, "Is this where they made the movie 'Silence of the Lambs?'" He thought that this convict was Hannibal Lecter.

A typical day started with breakfast at 6:30 a.m. There is nothing much to do for a convict who has a life sentence. A lifer is not eligible for certain jobs or trades because of the high security required for high custody convicts. I was incarcerated for three years and eight months. I received a job four months prior to my release.

On my yard, there were approximately four hundred three strike cases. Most of the men were not optimistic about getting out of prison. However, they were more concerned about when they would get a job so that they could come outside on weekends.

After returning from breakfast, the three strike inmate is placed in his cell until the yard is open. If you were assigned a job or trade, you would begin your routine. As three strikers, there were mostly no jobs available for us. The jobs were taken by inmates with a lower custody level requirement. A three striker's name is placed on a waiting list, it could take as long as four years for a job to be available. Therefore, working is not an option for a lifer.

After the yard has been run, you are let out for the dayroom to shower and watch a little television. At exactly 11:15 a.m. the dayroom and the yard are closed, after which you return to your cell for inmate count. The count usually clears about 12:15 p.m. You are then released for yard time. The weight pile is stripped of all the weights. The grass area is off limits to inmates. Only eight inmates are allowed per table. There are only three tables on the yard. Most convicts just stand around and talk because there is no place to sit. We plot and swap legal knowledge. Yardtime is over at 3:15 p.m. and your activity is over until the next day.

If you are not working or assigned a job or trade, then you are not permitted to go on the yard on Saturdays and Sundays. You are allowed two hours of dayroom time. You cannot come out at night. You cannot go out on holidays. You are allowed one telephone call per month. The telephone calls are run by privilege cards. Hell, everything is run by this card — it's the Gold Card of prison. The three strike inmate who cannot get a job is only entitled to one telephone call per month. As a three striker, you cannot come out on weekends and you cannot come out at nights, so when do you get the opportunity to make your one and only call per month? Like Keith Sweat said, "Make it last."

The prison authority makes it a point to place you as far away from your family as possible. Telephone calls and visitation from family and friends help to stimulate one's mind. The intent is to kill your mind so that you cannot think. Can you imagine what could happen if life inmates really started thinking and using their creative minds? Could this be the reason that life inmates are not given jobs or trades? Is four years the time needed to kill their minds and their hope?

The prison staff tries to press an inmate's patience. They know that they can push you around. After all, what can you do? They have you to abuse for life, and if you assault them they get a long sick leave.

A word regarding school and trade. I really don't know whether the state prison administration is out-slicking the prison auditors and inspectors or not. Could they be in cahoots together?

Auditors came down to the state prison every year for inspections. Whenever the inspectors were scheduled to come, classrooms would be opened up. The classroom may be for a computer class, but there is not one computer in it. While the auditors are present, it is set up to make believe that there is a legitimate class taking place. As soon as the inspectors/auditors complete their jobs, it becomes business as usual, and the inmates are back where they were before, the same routine - walking a straight line to eat. A line is approximately two feet wide.

CHAPTER

3

STRESS AND HASSLES
FOR VISITORS

Visitors are hassled. It appears as though the visiting guards are trained to try and discourage one's family from coming to visit. In Lancaster, there are four different yards -- Yards A - D. There is only one bus to shuttle everyone. The bus takes the first fifty, then the next fifty, etc. This process could take a visitor two hours just to get on the bus. This does not include the time it takes one to get into the yard to wait for the transportation bus that takes you to see the inmates.

Once the visitor has arrived by bus to the unit that houses the inmate, there is an additional thirty minutes to an hour wait for the inmate to come to you. By the time the inmate reaches the visitor, the visitor has already made up his/her mind that he/she will not be coming back. Therefore, you had better eat with them as though this is the last supper. Remember, you may never eat with them again.

A person visiting inmates should check prior to the visit regarding colors of clothing that are not permitted. Many times visitors are not permitted to visit after driving hundreds of miles and waiting hours in line because of the color they are wearing. A visitor must leave her purse in the automobile. You can only carry with you your California picture I.D. or driver's license.

It is important to inform your family and friends of this red tape in order to avoid hassles and disappointments. Keep in mind that visitors are made to feel humiliated. They are truly going out of their way to visit you. So be mindful how you treat them, regardless of what is happening to you.

CHAPTER

4

A MOTHER'S STORY

Melvin is my only son. He is my first born. I birthed him when I was fifteen years of age. He has had his share of challenges with the law and crime.

I remember visiting Melvin while he was incarcerated prior to his March 1994 framed conviction. I started to cry during one of my visits. Melvin said to me, "Mom, if you do the crime, you have to do the time." Not once did he ever complain or express anger or sadness when he was jailed for a crime that he committed.

In March of 1994, a friend of mine saw my son Melvin on the evening news. The news reporter stated that my Melvin was a runaway parolee who had now been arrested. I called Melvin's parole officer. I knew that Melvin was in Fresno with his parole officer's permission. He had written documents for proof. The parole officer said to me, "This is a mistake, and I will have it straightened out so don't you worry." I called him the second day after the event. He continued to assure me that he would handle it. I spoke to the parole officer on the third day. He said to me, "I did not tell you that I knew Melvin's whereabouts." I could not believe what my ears were hearing. I knew then that this time my son was in deep trouble.

My son gave the arresting officer the document which verified the fact that he had permission to be in Fresno. However, this important document came up missing. Somehow there must have been a righteous one among the police officers, because the document showed back up in Melvin's court file six months later. This document is very much related to the framing of my son; however, I cannot discuss it further at this time for legal reasons.

A mother can live with her son doing a life sentence for a crime which he has committed. Oh, how bad it hurts when your child faces a life sentence for a crime that you, know without a doubt that your child did not commit. How I lived and did not die is far beyond my understanding. When I would go to visit my son Melvin, the prison staff tried to make me, feel like a low-class criminal. They hassle you so badly that you hate to even go back to visit again. You know you must go back to see your child in spite of the abuse. After waiting for hours to see my son, I was told that I could not go in to see him because my dress had a buckle fastener on the back. I pleaded with them to cut the buckle off for me, but they would not do it.

I had to go to the mall to buy another dress. This left me only thirty minutes to visit my son upon my return. I had a problem visiting another time because Melvin's four year old daughter was wearing a dress with no sleeves on a hot summer day.

My emotional distress began to cause physical illness. I became diabetic and hypertensive. I became obsessed with the thought of my death and my son's death. I would think, if I die, will Melvin be allowed to come to my funeral? Will he die while in prison and I will have to go to get him? I kept searching for the pieces of the puzzle.

The entire three years and eight months that my son

was incarcerated, I was incarcerated too. I had to call his attorney on his behalf so many times. When he was upset, I was upset. I cried enough tears for every mother in the world who could not cry.

Most of the time when a young Black male is in prison, he only has his family. All his homies call you to inquire about his status. They cannot visit for the following reasons:

> Prior arrest record
>
> Improper identification
>
> Fear of being arrested themselves
>
> Fear of being identified with the inmate

The list goes on and on.

My son has been emotionally damaged. The thought of having been framed, and the thought of the pain that I have suffered, is too much for him to bear. We both hurt deeply. It is hard for us to put this behind us. The thought of my son's property being taken away from him on a false charge, and his not being allowed to go before the judge to request the return of his property, hurts us both deeply. His three strike conviction was reversed, however; they kept the property that had been taken away from him.

Melvin is blessed because he was able to return home to a mother, a stepfather, a grandmother and sisters who love him. I pray that every mother who has a child in prison will keep the faith as they work towards having their child return home. If your child tells you that he/she is innocent, believe him/her until proven guilty in your mind. Do not allow the media to force you to see your child from their viewpoint. Please see your child as to what he/she can become instead of what he/she is now.

If it had not been for my mother and God, I don't think I would be here to share my story. My mother told me to say these words everyday: "God grant me the serenity to accept the things I cannot change, the courage to change the things I can, and the wisdom to know the difference."

CHAPTER

I KEPT THE FAITH

Now faith is the substance of things hoped for, the evidence of things not seen (Hebrews 11:1). I continued praying to God daily. I began talking to him just like he was an ordinary man sitting next to me. I said to him, "Look-a-here God, I really need you now. I have done many terrible things in my life, but God, this time I was framed and wrongly arrested." I kept the faith in God and I kept the faith in myself. I asked God every day to strengthen my faith.

Oh, how I wish that I could turn back the hands of time so that I could take my mother out of her misery. My mother suffered so much pain. My life sentencing not only took my life; but it took my mother's life too. My family was not locked up but they were doing the time with me.

I kept praying that I would not have to hear about my mother dying while I was in prison. I was also praying that she did not have to get the news one day that I had died in prison. Those thoughts kept haunting me over and over again.

I was grieved over my mother's health. She appeared to have aged so much as a result of my being in jail. It was very plain to see that it had taken a toll on her quality of life and her health. I had to be strong. If I had shown any weakness, it would have drained her of any and all hope.

I kept telling my mother that I would not be kept in prison the rest of my life behind this case. I told her that the two of us would eat breakfast at her table again. I asked my mother to keep the faith as I have kept the faith.

I kept the faith. I kept the faith. I kept the faith. I sometimes ask the question, "God, did you do it for me or did you do it only for my mother?" I raise this question because I know that I have not been good in God's sight. A still voice answered me, saying, "None is good but the Father God."

I Kept The Faith

I have never had that kind of faith before. I don't even know where this faith came from, but I do know one thing; I never lost the faith.

CHAPTER

6

MY JUNETEENTH &
4TH OF JULY

God works in mysterious ways! On April 28, 1997, a case similar to mine had been reversed by the Supreme Court. On April 28, 1997, a decision was made that had positive implications for my case. Ain't God good?

The good news came to me via my appeal attorney. He told me that the ACLU had taken a case to the United States Supreme Court, and its decision was favorable for my case.

The following is the Supplemental Letter Brief re Oral Argument for my case:

May 28, 1997

Clerk

Court of Appeal, 5th District

P. O. Box 45013

Fresno, CA 93718

Re: People v. Farmer, F023554

        Supplemental Letter Brief re Oral Argument

[To the Clerk:]

Pursuant to your letter of May 22, 1997, appellant submits the instant supplemental letter brief with respect to recent authorities not included in the written briefs.

Issue I (whether exigent circumstances excused police non-compliance with the knock-notice rule):

1. On April 28, 1997, the United States Supreme Court rejected a "blanket exception" to knock-notice for an "entire category of criminal activity [ ]" (felony drug cases). (Richards v. Wisconsin (1997) ___ U.S. ___ (97 Daily Journal D.A.R. 5324, 5325]. The Supreme Court expressed two "serious concerns": the "considerable overgeneraliza-

tion" in the drug exception, and the threat that crime-category exceptions, such as armed robbery, would render the knock-notice requirement "meaningless." (Id. At 5326.) The court reiterated the basic test: "In order to justify a 'no-knock' entry, the police must have a reasonable suspicion that knocking and announcing their presence, under the particular circumstances, would be dangerous or futile, or that it would inhibit the effective investigation of the crime by, for example, allowing the destruction of evidence." (Ibid.)

2. On August 2, 1996, the Ninth Circuit held the knock-notice rule violated in United States v. Ramirez (9th Cir. 1996) 91 F.3d 1297. The fact-based explanation follows: "[The householders themselves presented no known danger. If he was there, Shelby [the subject of the arrest warrant] might wish to escape, but the phalanx of already positioned officers on hand made escape unlikely. Moreover, there was no specific evidence that Shelby was armed, that he would use firearms against the officers, or that when he was faced with a show of force he would do anything violent at all. Also, before the break-in nothing developed on the scene which would have added to the circumstances already

known and, thus, raise them to a higher degree of exigency."
(Id. at 1302.) In reviewing Ninth Circuit case law, the court
noted another case finding no exigency "after the police
heard a little noise, even though an occupant was a drug
dealer who had a prior conviction for armed robbery." (Id.
at 1301, citing United States v. Mendonsa (9th Cir. 1993)
989 F.2d 366, 370-371.)

3. On April 7, 1997, the Ninth Circuit found noncompliance
excused in the context of a civil lawsuit against law enforcement authorities. (Thompson v. Mahre (9th Cir. 1997) 110
F.3d 716 [97 Daily Journal D.A.R. 4501].) The issue in this
civil case was "whether a reasonable officer could have
believed that forcible entry was necessary to protect the officers against armed resistance and protect against destruction
of evidence." (97 D.A.R. at 4504.) The court relied on the
following principles: "Where a defendant is 'in possession
of narcotics, which could be quickly and easily destroyed,'
and the facts indicate that 'he might well have been expect-
ing the police,' the special exigency of preventing destruction of evidence may excuse failure to knock and announce.
[Citation.] Likewise, where the police officers reasonably
believe themselves to be endangered because the defendant

had previously expressed willingness to use firearms against police and was known to have them, the exigency exception applies. [Citations.]" (Id. at 4503.)

The court then highlighted the key facts supporting its conclusion of reasonableness: "It is undisputed that the officers had probable cause to believe that Deshetres had methamphetamine in the house. That was the basis for the search warrant. If he knew the police were coming, he could flush it down the toilet. It is also undisputed that Sergeant Steen had reason to believe that Deshetres was a career criminal who had once robbed a narcotics dealer with a gun and taken a hostage, and had once been reaching for a gun while being arrested. The police also had reason to think that the driver of the white pickup truck had tipped Deshetres off, so he had additional time to destroy evidence and arm himself." (Ibid.)

4. On October 31, 1996, the Third District rejected a claim of knock-notice violation in People v. Zabelle (1996) 50 Cal.App.4th 1282. The narcotics officer saw, through an open hotel room door, the apparently sleeping defendant in

an odd fetal position next to what appeared to be heroin. Suspecting an overdose, the officer went in to investigate. He said nothing "because he was concerned for his own safety: he could not see defendant's hands and did not know what might be in his hands." (Id. at 1285.) The Court of Appeal found that the officer reasonably "limited the potential for violence by entering to a place where he could put his hands on defendant before waking him." (Id. at 1287.)

I was scheduled for oral argument on June 12, 1997 in the California Court of Appeals. The scheduled hearing would render a decision as to whether I would be a free man or whether I would spend the rest of my life in prison.

I called my attorney after the hearing. My attorney explained to me that the Attorney General had not shown up to argue the case on behalf of the state. This is rare and almost unprecedented. In my mind I was thinking, I have it made if they follow the law. My reasoning was that if the Attorney General had not contested my conviction, then how could the state hold me in prison? I was told that a decision would be made in approximately ninety days.

Shortly after Juneteenth and a little before the July 4th, I was called from my cell to pick up "legal mail." This was not just any piece of mail. My fate would be decided in this letter that I was about to receive. This piece of mail carried my fate. I was so afraid. My heart started skipping beats. My stomach felt like a ball of fire was inside it.

Everyone in the building was quiet; they too awaited my fate. They all knew that I actually had a shot at going home. I was shaking and trembling when the letter was handed to me. Upon opening my legal mail, the first thing I saw on the letter was "We Won" written in big letters. I did not read any further, I just hollered out, "I'm gone, I'm gone, I am going home." This is the letter that I received:

June 30, 1997

Melvin E. Farmer, C-10562

44700 60th Street. West

Lancaster, CA 93536-7620

Re: People v. Farmer appeal, No. F023554
        Madera County No. 11941

Dear Mr. Farmer:

WE WON!

Yes, it's true. I'm enclosing the opinion of the Court of Appeal, reversing the judgment in your case. They agreed that the evidence should have been thrown out because of the illegal search, which means, of course, that you never should have gone to trial.

I wish I could say that it was all over now. But the court's decision isn't final yet. The Attorney General has until July 10 to file a petition for rehearing in the same Court of Appeal. (I don't think they will file such a petition, and if they do, I'm pretty sure the court would deny it.) And they have until August 4 to file a petition for review in the California Supreme Court, trying to interest them in hearing this appeal. I think it's a little more likely that the AG will file a petition for review. (I'll send you a copy if that happens.) And although I don't think it would be granted, it would postpone things for a while. The Supreme Court has up to 90 days to decide whether to grant review. If they do, then there's another round of briefing, argument, etc., over the next year or two. If they deny review, then the Court of Appeal decision stands.

So here's what we're looking at: If nothing more is filed, the Court of Appeal decision will become final on July 25, and around August 25 the Court of Appeal will issue a "remittitur"-- basically, an order sending the case back to the superior court. If the AG files a petition for review, and if it's not granted by the Supreme Court, the remittitur would be issued later -- maybe as late as the beginning of November.

Either way, once the remittitur is issued, you're supposed to be sent back to Madera County for a court appearance. (I'll send a copy of the Court of Appeal opinion to your lawyer there, so he knows what's going on and can make sure you get back to court.) In court, unless the DA has some other evidence available in the same case (which seems impossible; the whole case was based on the evidence seized in the raid on the house), the prosecution would be dismissed. At that point, unless you're still doing time on a parole revocation or something like that, you should just walk. As in: Free. Of course, that "free" comes with a lot of baggage. You still have strike convictions which can be used to give you a life term for any new felony -- including petty theft with a prior, assault, burglary, etc. Obviously, whatever you can do to stay away from the criminal justice system, you should do.

Anyway, that's a little premature right now. We've won an enormous battle, but the war's not over yet. I'll let you know as soon as I have more news. In the meantime, congratulations!

I went to my homeboy's cell, Mike Wilson, and told him the news. He said, "Man, you lying. No one has ever gone home on a three strike case on a straight out reversal." I threw the letter under his cell door. I then went to my different homies' cells shouting the good news, "I'm going home." They were all congratulating me on going home.

In the midst of my joy, an officer was there trying to have me locked up. He said that I wasn't supposed to be out. Oh, but I was, and I had proof.

I refused to be locked up. According to prison protocol, I was to immediately return to my cell after receiving mail. I asked the officer who was in charge of the telephone to allow me to call my mother. I was determined that this night my mother was going to sleep in peace. After some delay, I was allowed to call my mother. She asked what happened? I said to her, "They denied me." She lost her breath, and I then shouted, "Mother, I am coming home!" She hollered out, "Melvin, my son, is coming home. Thank God!" I cautioned my mother that we still had a while to go. I explained that the Attorney General could appeal to a higher court and they had approximately sixty days to do so. But as it stood right now, I said to her, "I am a free man." To hear the joy in my mother's voice once again was a sweet melody to my ears. Many thoughts had flashed through my mind — Would I have to tell my mom again that I wouldn't be coming home? Could she live through this? Not only was I concerned about the welfare of my mother, but my daughter's hugs and kisses were also of great concern. The hardest pain to bear was the thought of never spending time in the outside world with my daughter.

My daughter, Melanie was three-years-old at the time of my arrest. This was my only daughter of three children. I was more disturbed about being taken away from my daughter than from having my life taken away from me via imprisonment.

My mother faithfully brought my daughter to visit me regularly. Melanie would ask me what are you doing in this place. Prison was known to her as this place. She could not get the answer from me nor my family. I knew the answer, but I could not tell her why I was in this place.

Now that my daughter and I have reconnected, she is up and down. She is more down than up. For four years she had only known me from that place. It is so wonderful to be able to hug and kiss my daughter and to give her the love that she needs from me, her father.

I could not sleep that night. While lying in my cell, I said to my cellie, "I have talked to everyone in here and not once have I said, 'Thank you Jesus'. I have thanked everyone but Jesus, and I am not too ashamed to say 'Thank you Lord'." My cellie told me that it wouldn't hurt. While lying on my back, I looked up toward heaven and I uttered these words, "Thank You, Lord, for giving me my freedom and my life back." The very next breath that I took after saying those words felt like spring-fresh air. A calmness came over my entire body. I felt a peace which I had not felt in almost four years.

This was my personal Juneteenth, this was my July 4th. As much as I have tried to convey my feelings to you, I feel that I cannot do it well enough for you to really see the picture clearly. The following is a letter I received from my attorney:

August 5, 1997

Melvin E. Farmer, C-10562

44750 60th St. West

Lancaster, CA 93536-7620

Re: People v. Farmer appeal, No. F023554 (Madera No. 11941)

Dear Mr. Farmer:

As you know, the Attorney General had until August 4 to file a petition for review in the California Supreme Court. That was yesterday, and the clerk just told me no such petition was filed. So the decision is now final. Once again, congratulations.

Next: The remittitur should be issued around August 25, with the case then going back to the superior court for further proceedings consistent with the order of reversal. As I've told you, given the fact that all the evidence in the case must be suppressed, there would appear to be only one possible proceeding: dismissal.

I've written to both the county clerk and Mr. Richter, your trial attorney, pointing out that soon you should be sent back to Madera County for a court appearance. (I'm enclosing a copy of the letter to the clerk.) I'd appreciate it if you would write to me and let me know what happens after that. (I'm also enclosing a self-addressed, stamped envelope.)

Once again, please remember that those "strike" convictions aren't going away. As long as the three strike law stays in effect, you're subject to the same 34-to-life term for any new felony. I wish you luck with any civil proceedings, according to what you told me on the phone. But most importantly, I hope you're able to stay out of the clutches of the criminal justice system. Given the terrible odds against defendants winning appeals, you can't count on being able to do it again.

I'm glad to have represented you in this appeal. Because it is now over, though, I'm no longer your attorney. The trial court transcripts are your property, so I am sending them in a separate box.

Best of luck with everything!

CHAPTER

7

MY JOYS AND FEARS

The joy I felt is unexplainable. I went to the yard the next day after receiving my "you won" letter. I was the talk of the day. Everyone knew that my going home would be a first - no one had been released in the two years since I had been there.

As I rejoiced out loud, I felt a cold chill run down my back. I sensed that it was not in good taste to rejoice in the presence of men who had life sentences. How do you talk about going home to men with life sentences and no hope? You don't. If it is not brought up in conversation by another convict, protocol is to keep your mouth shut.

The joy is that I can go to church, spend time with

my daughter and see my mother smile. The joy is that I can bring comfort to other parents whose sons have a life sentence. I can help make the public aware that inmates need their help. I am not talking about financial help. I am talking about genuine interest in what is happening to the people in prison. There is seldom a positive response to the many cries for help in combating the inhumane treatment that inmates are subjected to on a daily basis. Few of you know what that treatment is like. One thing for sure is that what prison administrators tell you is not anything near the truth.

I have peaks of joy and I have many fears. The fear is that I could be framed or set-up again. I am afraid everyday. In my heart, I know that I should not rest until these men who framed me are held accountable. Yet my mother gets upset at the thought of my pursuing the matter. I have not been able to obtain an attorney for this case.

I am a free prisoner. I did not bring home the joy that I anticipated for my mother. She continues to have sleepless nights. You see, my mother's fears are a result of her knowing the truth about my being framed and wrongly arrested. When she is afraid, it makes me fear. When there is no joy for my mother, there is no joy for me.

I was given a thirty-four years to life sentence handed down by man. Only God could have gotten me out of this situation. I don't believe he did this for me, for no reason or purpose. I feel in my heart that he wants these officers brought to justice before they do the same to someone else.

One day I have joy; the next day I do not. One day I have fear; the next day I do not. I continue to search for mental and emotional freedom for myself and my family.

CHAPTER

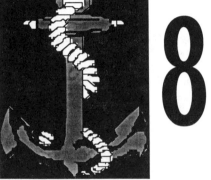

8

A CHARGE TO KEEP

In 1994, the criminals who were breaking into people's houses should have been breaking down the voting polls to vote against the three strike initiative. The three strike law is no joke. Men and women are sentenced for life as a result of retroactive crimes committed. I think the public was tricked this time. Most people who voted in favor of the three strike law were not aware that it also covered non-violent crimes.

Inmates are confined to an 8' x 10' stand-up grave (called cell). Most of their hours are spent rotting away like wood in salt water.

When it was certain that I was going home, I asked

the inmates with petty crime convictions to write down all their information for me. I promised them that I would try my best to speak up for them. Many of these guys have given up. They have no faith in the court system.

I pledged a solemn oath to the brothers that I would do my best to expose what is really going on with the inmates and how their lives, have been taken away by the tricky three strike law. Some of the inmates said to me, "Melvin, are you really going to try to do something to help us?" The look that I saw on their faces that day is the look that haunts me every day and every night.

I don't know how to help these men. I am carrying a heavy burden upon my shoulders. Every day I ask God to show me the way to help those inmates that I left behind.

CHAPTER

9

A CLOSE-UP LOOK AT THE THREE STRIKE LAW

Important Features of the Three Strike Law:

Anyone with two serious or violent prior felonies, or "strikes," faces 25 years to life with any third felony. This means serving a minimum of 20 years.

A second strike means double the sentence that would be imposed for a first offense.

Prior offenses countable as strikes may be dismissed by prosecutors to avoid punishment that is out of proportion to the offense and the overall background of the offender.

Judges are granted no discretion in dismissing strikes or pronouncing sentences, but some are exercising it anyway.

Plea bargaining is not allowed on the second or third strike.

What counts as a strike?

Serious Felonies

- Voluntary manslaughter
- Mayhem
- Kidnapping
- Carjacking
- Assault with intent to rape or rob
- Assault with a deadly weapon on a police officer
- Rape
- Forcible sodomy
- Lewd act on a child
- Forcible oral copulation
- Forcible penetration by a foreign object
- Arson
- Residential burglary
- Grand theft firearm
- Assault by life prisoner on non-inmate
- Assault with a deadly weapon by inmate
- A prisoner holding a hostage
- Personal use of a deadly weapon

- Personal use of a firearm
- Personal infliction of great bodily harm
- Exploding destructive device to injure
- Exploding destructive device to murder
- Exploding destructive device with mayhem/great bodily harm
- Selling/furnishing drugs to minor
- Certain drug conspiracies with a minor
- Any felony punishable by death or life
- Attempt of any listed crime except assaults
- Violent Felonies
- Murder
- Voluntary manslaughter
- Forcible rape
- Forcible sodomy
- Forcible oral copulation
- Lewd act on a child
- Robbery
- Any felony punishable by death or life in prison
- Any felony with great bodily injury
- Any felony with firearm use
- Residential robbery with weapon use

- Arson with great bodily injury
- Forcible penetration by a foreign object
- Attempted murder
- Exploding destructive device to murder
- Kidnapping for child molestation
- Kidnapping a child
- Continuous sexual abuse of a child
- Carjacking with weapon use

The three strike law was enacted by Assembly Bill 971 in March 1994. This was an emergency measure, as alleged by California Governor Pete Wilson. Was there really an emergency or was the governor in a tight political race? The three strike law was sold to the public under the pretense that it would rid the state of the violent criminals as well as the repeat offenders (that was the big print). The small print stated that anyone with one or more priors shall be eligible for double their sentence if they have one prior violent or serious crime, and twenty-five-years-to-life if they have two or more prior convictions.

The habitual offenders' law, of which most people have little knowledge , was already in effect prior to the three strike law. The habitual offenders law reads as follows:

HABITUAL OFFENDERS (Punishable Offenses)

An habitual offender must be punished with life imprisonment, either with or without possibility of parole, unless the greater punishment of death or imprisonment for life without possibility of parole may be imposed, as described below. An habitual offender is one who

(1)   Has been convicted of a felony involving the infliction of great bodily injury or the personal use of force likely to produce great bodily injury; and

(2)   Has served two or more prior separate prison terms for:

(a)   Any specified felony;...

(b)   Any felony involving great bodily injury; or

(c)   Any felony punishable by death or life imprisonment with or without possibility of parole.

However, if the offender has not been in prison custody or has not committed an offense resulting in a felony conviction for 10 years, the earlier offenses may not be used as prior separate prison terms. A commitment to the California Youth Authority following conviction for a felony constitutes a prior prison term for purposes of the habitual offender law.

If the defendant has served two prior separate prison terms, the defendant is punishable by life imprisonment with the possibility of parole. However, the defendant is not eligible for release on parole for 20 years, or the term determined by the court under Penal Code Section 1170 for the underlying conviction, including any applicable enhancement or any period described by Penal Code Section 190 or 346, whichever is greatest, subject to reduction for postsentence conduct credit.

Under the habitual criminal law, one's arrest must be for a violent or serious offense. Whereas, with the three strike law, any arrest and conviction triggers the three strike mandatory sentencing. Since the habitual criminal law includes all violent and serious felon offenders, the difference between the two is that the three strike law includes the non-violent, non-serious and petty crime offenders. It does not take a rocket scientist to see that the three strike law was designed to line the pockets of those with a vested interest in the prison system market. The three strike law guarantees a return on investment for those large corporations involved in the new prison industry. Life sentencing ensures the stability of the prison industry and makes it more attractive for investors.

CHAPTER

10

THREE STRIKE MYTHS
AND REALITIES

MYTH: My priors are old; they can't be used.

REALITY: Any prior before or after 1994 can and will be used against you.

MYTH: I must commit a violent or serious offense.

REALITY: Any felony charge that leads to a conviction makes you eligible for the three strike law.

MYTH: I'm only charged with a nonviolent offense; three strikes is for violent offenders.

REALITY: If you have one or more violent or serious priors, it doesn't matter if your third strike is not a felony.

MYTH: I'll just take a deal if I'm convicted.

REALITY: There are no deals allowed. Either you beat your case or suffer the fate of many — life in prison.

MYTH: My priors are from my juvenile days. They can't be used.

REALITY: Juvenile priors, if they're violent or serious, will be used against you.

MYTH: My priors are in another state and can't be used.

REALITY: Your priors can be used from Timbuktu. If the court can prove that they exist, they can be used.

MYTH: I took a deal on my priors and therefore wasn't convicted in court.

REALITY: Any felony to which you pled guilty is usable, even though they didn't tell you at the time that you could get life for it twenty years later, and in some cases beyond.

MYTH: I was convicted of only one crime but pled guilty to two or three. That means that I only have one prior.

REALITY: Even though you pled guilty to one crime, it

was broken down into three. You have three priors over that one case, and they will be used against you.

THE LAW:

Anyone with two or more serious or violent prior felonies or strikes faces 25- years-to-life with any third conviction. A minimum of 20 years must be served before becoming eligible for parole.

A second strike means double the sentence that would be imposed for a first offense. In other words, if you receive a sentence of 5 years, it would double to 10 years at eighty percent.

A strike is any serious or violent offense for which you were convicted prior to 1994.

Any arrest triggers the three strike law and makes you eligible for a life sentence.

Each case for which you were charged under three strikes will run consecutive with each other. In other words, if you catch a case and there are four different charges, then each charge carries a life term and will be served one after the other. Your total term with the four convictions will add up to 100-years-to-life at 80 percent.

A person convicted under three strikes must be sent to prison.

CHAPTER

11

CONCLUSION

Conclusion

I am by no means a saint. I am a human being. I have compassion for those who are victimized.

I am not a rocket scientist; however, I know that the three strike law is not good for this nation. The prison economic scheme is going to cause America to be educationally deprived and financially bankrupt. Justice must work for all of us, if America wants to have peace.

Isn't there something wrong with a country where doctors, lawyers, politicians, judges, etc., are scheming to make a decent living? Is anybody awake in the house? The three strike law must be changed immediately. I am encouraging everybody who respects law and justice to join the organization that is fighting against the three strike law.

Inmates need your help. When I say help, I am talking about genuine interest in what is happening to them. Their hearts are turned to rock-hard anger. Do inmates deserve the inhumane treatment that they are subjected to daily?

Many Black professionals are discussing the plight of Blacks and Black males in particular. They are holding open radio and television forums. They talk good talk, but when the sun sets, they are resting peacefully in their fabulous homes.

If you really want to discuss the Black man and Black woman's dilemma, you should talk to them first. How many of those talking have visited a prison, a jail, or even juvenile hall?

An article in *EM Magazine* made the following observation: Statistics show that 30% of Black men between the ages of 18 and 24 are in the criminal justice system. In Washington, DC, a reported 50% of Black men between the ages of 18 and 24 are caught up in the criminal justice system. Try to envision Washington, DC's Black male population ten years from now with the three strike law in force.

Conclusion

Blacks account for 12% of the U.S. population, and approximately 13% of all monthly drug users, yet 35% of people arrested for drug possession are Black. 55% of those convicted are Black and 75% of those incarcerated are Black. Drug usage between races is not unequal. What's up? According to research, most drug abusers in America are White, but more Blacks are locked up.

It is important that the public become aware of issues that are causing people of color to become locked up for life over petty crimes.

I am not asking anyone for any money. I am asking you to investigate the prison and the justice systems for yourself. I am not asking you to believe me; you may decide I have no credibility because I was once a criminal. Go see for yourself.

Please do not allow all those men, women and even children to rot away in prison for petty crimes. Remember, the life you save may be your own.

BIBLIOGRAPHY

1. Ebony Man Magazine: December, 1997

2. Emerge Magazine: October 1997.

3. Hutchinson, Earl Ofari, Ph.D. The Assassination of The Black Male Image, Los Angeles: Middle Passage Press, 1994.

4. Jefferson, Roland S., M.D. The School on 103rd Street. New York: W.W. Norton and Company, Inc., 1997.

5. Milligan, Rosie Dr. Nigger, Please. Los Angeles: Professional Business Consultants, 1994.

BOOKS AVAILABLE THROUGH
Milligan books
By Dr. Rosie Milligan

The New Slave Ship $10.00

Juror $10.95

Birth of A Christian $9.95

Rootin' For The Crusher, $12.99

Temptation - $12.95

Satisfying the Blackwoman sexually Made Simple - $14.95

Satisfying the Blackman Sexually Made simple - $14.95

Negroes-Colored People-Blacks-African-Americans in America- $13.95

Starting A Business Made Simple - $20.00

Getting Out of Debt Made Simple - $20.00

Nigger, Please -14.95

A Resource Guide for African American Speakers & Writers - 49.95

...............................**Order Form**...................................

Mail Check or Money Order to: 1425 W. Manchester, suite B, Los Angeles, CA 90047

Name_____Date_____
Address_____
City_____State _____Zip Code_____
Day Telephone _____
Eve Telephone _____
Name of book(s) _____
Sub Total $ _____
Sales Tax (CA) Add 8.25% $ _____
Shipping & Handling $3.00 $ _____
Total Amount Due $ _____
❑ Check   ❑ Money Order
❑ Visa   ❑ Master Card   Ex. Date _____

Credit Card No. _____
Driver's License No. _____

_____   _____
Signature   Date